Snails have no reverse gear!
Eddie Askew

*Lord, help me to realise
that whatever life may bring today
it comes wrapped up in you.
And that should be enough.*

Foreword

Within a few minutes of wondering what to write in this foreword, I am transported into the sunshine and warmth of Purulia, India. Once again, I am a small child in a big garden saying hello, with my dad, to our pet monkey, Squeak. He loved my dad and seemed happiest sitting on Dad's head grooming him. I fondly remember his antics, especially when he ran off towards the roof of our garage with a goose egg under his arm, much like a rugby player making a dash for the try line.

Dad loved animals. We had dogs, cats, guinea pigs, mice, a peacock, geese and monkeys over the years. He wanted to build a zoo of sorts for the leprosy patients as he had spotted a small bear cub for sale in the local market. My mum didn't share his enthusiasm. "And what will you do when it's full grown?" she asked. The subject was never mentioned again, but he engendered in my sister and me a great love for animals of any kind. He taught us to recognise birds by sight or by their song, probably because it distracted us from the terrible insistent rising call of the aptly named 'brain fever bird', which sang in the hot weather.

Now, as adults, we have very willingly passed this legacy on to our children together with Dad's made-up stories of the Silver Grey monkey, whose adventures were only ever shared on a Sunday morning before breakfast. And there are memories of an invisible donkey called 'Neddie Wiffle', who lived under our dining table. He was so real that we brought him back to England with us when we settled back here.

So Dad, you've done your work well. Your grandchildren regularly rescue birds, look out for stray cats, feed sugar water to exhausted bees, and continue to love our pets with the commitment that you taught us. Thank you. Life is so much the richer for it.

My hope is that you, the reader, will enjoy these thoughts as much as we did.

Jenny Hawke, February 2018

4

Snails have no reverse gear!

Blessed are those who find wisdom,
those who gain understanding…
Proverbs 3:13

I made a startling discovery the other day. It may not change the world but it's
this: snails don't have a reverse gear. I went to the greenhouse to water my
tomato plants. The watering can was heavy, full of water, but when I picked it up
and tilted it, only a trickle of water came through. I put the can down, unscrewed
the spout and held it up to the light. It was almost totally blocked by something
dark. I poked a cane down through the narrow end and out dropped a snail.
A dead snail.

Attracted by the damp it must have crawled in and up the spout. Unfortunately
watering can spouts taper and get smaller nearer the outlet. The snail went in as
far as it could go, then got jammed. And that was that. There was no room to turn
and the snail had no reverse gear.

It made me think. Never put yourself into a situation you can't back out of. Bad
grammar, but you see what I mean. People argue and, in the heat of the moment,
make statements they can't justify, and then find they can't back away. Too
embarrassing. They get aggressive, which makes things worse, and before you
know it World War Three has broken out. Or nearly so.

Take time to listen to what the other person's saying. Put yourself in their place and
don't push too hard or you may get stuck without any chance of backing away.
Leave room for understanding and keep the channels of communication unblocked.
Remember the snail.

Lord, it may be asking a lot of you, but help me to think before I speak, and then not to say too much.

Extract from Love is a Wild Bird, *first published 2003.*

The beauty of butterflies

That which was from the beginning, which we have heard, which we have seen with our eyes, which we have looked at and our hands have touched - this we proclaim concerning the Word of life.
1 John 1:1

A neighbour of mine took his family for a week's holiday on the canal. They hired a narrow boat. The weather was kind, the landscape on the river banks green and gentle. The pace of life was slow, undemanding, apart from the locks which punctuated the journey with commas rather than full stops on the way.

A few days after their return he and I were both in our drives washing our cars. I asked him about the holiday. "Great," he said, "We relaxed, watched the life around us. One day we noticed butterflies on the river bank, and realised they were travelling faster than we were. It gave us a new perspective."

Life is fast these days. There's little time for anything but the immediate demands of work and daily living. The 'human' things are in danger of being squeezed out. A popular poet of my youth, W. H. Davies, wrote:
"What is this life if full of care, we have no time to stand and stare..."

He wasn't thinking of an aimless idleness where nothing registers, but of a long look which takes in the world around us. A look which wonders and delights in the intricate beauty of butterflies and all that nature offers. It may renew our perspective and help us understand that life is more than a mad rush from one commitment to another.

St. John links it to our spiritual awareness. "That which we have looked at," he says, and the word means gazed at, taken time over. Whether it's the river bank, butterflies or the revelation of God's love in Jesus Christ, we need to take time to consider it, absorb its beauty and reflect on how it can change our lives.

Extract from Slower than Butterflies, *first published 1997.*

Lord, give me the grace to pause, take breath and reassess just where I am, to find time to hear your voice in the quiet. ... And in the silence as the treadmill of my mind stops turning I'll hear you offering me Shalom. The peace that passes understanding. And then refreshed, my energy restored, I can begin again to live as you would have me live.

One small sparrow

Here is a boy with five small barley loaves and two small fish,
but how far will they go among so many?"
John 6:9

It was early morning. We were staying with friends and I was looking out over the garden from the bedroom window. The sky was clear and sunny. A good day, I thought. Then a sudden movement caught my eye. The telephone wire, stretched across the garden and anchored just below the window, was swaying.

There, just yards away, was a sparrow. He was perched on the wire, tail twitching as he kept his balance. I suppose he only weighed an ounce or so – or maybe I should say a few grams these days – but his coming had set the wire dancing. And when he flew off, as he did when I unthinkingly moved my hand, he set the wire dancing even more.

It was just a momentary thing but it made me realise that even a small event can have a significance far beyond itself. "Oh," we say, confronted by some world problem, "there's nothing I can do about it." And we turn away, feeling helpless. But, if we accept that we can do nothing, that's just what we'll achieve. Nothing. So let's try.

Say something, write to the papers, lobby your MP. Whatever it takes. Who knows, your weight may set the wires dancing. Maybe it won't, but at least you've tried and that has to be worth something. And it's the same with relationships. A friendly gesture, a welcoming word, may make someone else's day. It doesn't take an awful lot of energy to make the world dance – or at least our little part of it.

Lord, teach me to dance in the joy of your presence today.

Extract from Love is a Wild Bird, *first published 2003.*

11

Acrobatic squirrels

"In your anger do not sin."
Do not let the sun go down while you are still angry,
and do not give the devil a foothold.
Ephesians 4:26-27

Lovely little animals, squirrels. All those acrobatics as they try to reach the peanuts we hang out for the birds in the garden. They usually manage it too. And take the lot. But then they began to worry me. They started digging up and eating the tulip bulbs I'd planted in the autumn. I still forgave them. "Maybe I should have planted them deeper," I thought, but I wish now I'd done something to discourage them.

You see, the other day the burglar alarm went off for no apparent reason. I cleared it. Then it went off again, and again. Seven times in one afternoon. The engineer came, checked everything and found a broken wire in the loft. We looked at the wire more closely – toothmarks. Mice? Rats? No, a squirrel nesting in the loft and chewing through anything that got in its way.

I was told I'd better do something quick – the breeding season was beginning. I got onto a builder, but not before the squirrel had chewed through another wire and set the alarm off again. I won't bother you with the rest of the saga. The point is if I'd done something earlier about the squirrel the problem wouldn't have got so big. The word is, "Act now." And that goes for human relationships, not just squirrels.

When friendships go wrong, when there are family misunderstandings, don't let them go on. Do something to put them right. Don't wait for the other person. Make a move yourself. The Bible says, "Don't let the sun go down while you're still angry." Do something to put things right. That way quarrels are short circuited, friendships restored. Don't go on shouting. Show a bit of love. But maybe not so much to the squirrels.

Extract from Slower than Butterflies, *first published 1997.*

A time for action and a time to wait.
My problem, Lord, is knowing which is which.
Grace me with your wisdom,
a little is enough for now, and just a bit of understanding.
Help me to see each situation with your eyes
and act, when action's needed, with a sympathy
that can only come from you.

An armada of Canada geese

"Therefore I tell you, do not worry about your life, what you will eat or drink;
or about your body, what you will wear.
Is not life more than food, and the body more than clothes?
Look at the birds of the air; they do not sow or reap or store away in barns,
and yet your heavenly Father feeds them.
Are you not much more valuable than they?
Can any one of you by worrying add a single hour to your life?
Matthew 6:25–27

It was cold, down at the nature reserve. The sky was steel grey, clouds torn by
an almost gale-force wind. It ripped through the trees, scattering the last leaves.
The water was grey and ruffled. A great armada of Canada geese was in the water,
together with dozens of other waterbirds. They floated there, facing into the storm.

Their environment had suddenly become hostile, threatening. They didn't protest,
or run for cover. They didn't use up precious energy flying into it, or fighting it. They
faced into the wind, paddling quietly. They didn't try to make headway, but paddled
just enough to keep their direction and position in the water.

Maybe we can learn from the birds. Jesus thought so. They tell us of God's concern,
he said, and remind us that we achieve little by worrying. When the going gets tough,
the tough get going, says the cliché. I'm not sure that's always the best way. We're
not all as aggressive as that suggests. Another way is just to face the storm, and keep
position. Not scream and shout, not protest and ask what have I done to deserve
this, but just hold on to faith and wait for the wind to blow itself out. It will, because
the creator of the winds is stronger than the wind.

It may take time, but it works, and I don't remember ever seeing a Canada
goose with acute depression.

Extract from Facing the Storm, *first published 1989.*

Creator God, when the storms come, help me to hold on to my faith and wait for the wind to blow itself out.

Look at the birds.
That's what you said, Lord.

And there they are,
just getting on
with the business of living.
Being birds.
Facing the storm.

That's part of my problem, I reckon.
Not content to be me.
Wanting something different.
Creating my own tensions.
Piling up the building blocks of discontent.
Making my own high-rise apartments of unhappiness.
Isolating myself in anxiety.
Made worse
when the hand of reality gives it all a push,
and I sit,
a child in the ruins,
howling.

Help me understand, Lord,
that wherever I'm at,
you're there.
That you have something for me.
That you care.
As a hen gathers her chicks under her wings,
you said.

Nice picture, that.
Safe from the world,
warm, secure.
But chicks grow up,
and so must I.
Get out into the cold wind
of the world out there.

But knowing that your wings
are stronger than the storm.

I think I can live with that.

It's a bug's life

For when I am weak, then I am strong.
2 Corinthians 12:10

I saw something small moving across the carpet in the hall. It was just one of the many bugs and insects that crawl or fly into the house when we open up the doors and windows in summer. I don't like killing creatures unnecessarily if they're doing no harm; and when you look at them closely they're all breathtaking miracles of miniature design. I must admit I'm not so altruistic when the flying ants start but this was different. So I grabbed a bit of paper, gently picked up the bug and carried it out into the garden.

I shook the paper but the bug wouldn't let go, so I gave it an encouraging flick of the finger and away it sailed through the air. When it touched down, its legs were still moving and it crawled away without a pause as though nothing had happened.

"Wow," I thought, "if someone had thrown me through the air like that I'd be in no fit state to walk away." To me it would have been like falling off a cliff, a major disruption in my life. But the bug? Well, it just got on with the job of living. It goes with my best wishes, and I reckon it's got something to say to all of us.

Creator Lord, open my eyes to your presence in all created things,
however small, and help me learn
from their strength and perseverance.

Extract from Dabbling with Ducks, *first published 2007.*

Fly to freedom

*For the revelation awaits an appointed time...though it linger wait for it;
it will certainly come and will not delay.*
Habbakuk 2:3

It was early spring. I was working in the garden, moving a pile of old bricks rescued from when we repaved the driveway. Hidden in a space between two of the bricks I found a dusty, grey cocoon. Last autumn a caterpillar had fattened itself up by eating into my shrubbery. It had found somewhere to hide, spun its protection against the winter – and hibernated.

As I looked at it, it seemed dead, totally inert with nothing happening. But in the secrecy of the cocoon, changes were taking place. Gradually, quietly, mysteriously, the caterpillar inside was being transformed. In a few days, the restrictive cocoon would split and a new creature would emerge. A butterfly or moth – I can't identify cocoons – would unfold its wings and fly into a freedom it had never known. Its waiting time over.

I wonder sometimes about what really happened on the first Easter Saturday. I know about the drama of Good Friday and the joy of Easter Sunday, but what about the day in between? The day when nothing seemed to be happening. The day the disciples were mourning for what had been and didn't yet know what would be.

Even then, things were happening unseen and unknown in the cocoon of God's purposes. Events that would shake the world and change it more powerfully than anything else, events that would give us the freedom to live as nothing else could. All that was needed was time.

Waiting can be hard, but little happens without it.

Lord, let me glimpse your purpose in the mystery of life.
And when the mist descends, help me to wait in patience.

Extract from Talking with Hedgehogs, *first published 2001.*

Fighting the leaves

*'Love the Lord your God with all your heart and with all your soul
and with all your strength and with all your mind';
and 'Love your neighbour as yourself.'*
Luke 10:27

We acquired Milli, our new puppy, a Cavalier King Charles Spaniel, during the last days of autumn. She loves leaves. In her view, going into the garden has nothing to do with toilet training. It was just a glorious opportunity to fight the leaves as they dropped from the trees. First, she'd sniff at them as they lay quietly in corners but she was really waiting for the wind.

When it came, swirling the leaves, moving them, lifting them, she was ecstatic. Maybe she saw them as barbarian hordes to be attacked and repelled; she would leap and run and pounce on them. Sometimes it was just one particular leaf she'd follow and capture, then chew it to bits. It was fun to watch, although I'm sure there's a serious purpose behind it, an instinctive urge in her to practise and develop her agility and strength.

What impressed me most though, after the laughter, was the way she threw herself into the adventure. It was all or nothing. Fighting the leaves took all her attention, all her energy and commitment. I'm supposed to be training Milli, but I think she's training me. She's telling me that if I want to make a good job of all I do today I'd better use the same commitment and energy she uses. That goes for our friendships too.

And when it's all over, Milli knows just how to curl up and relax – on the sofa. I find that easier to do.

Lord of love and laughter, I give myself to you without reserve.
At least, that's what I aim to do. Give me a helping hand.

Extract from Chasing the Leaves, *first published 2003.*

Adopted by a lioness

The wolf will live with the lamb, the leopard will lie down with the goat... and the lion will eat straw like the ox.
Isaiah 11:6-7

I wonder if you saw a press report about a lioness who adopted an orphaned oryx – a small antelope – and mothered it. The paper had a picture of the two of them together, lioness and antelope, walking through the scrub in Kenya.

Usually, in the lion's economy, antelopes are viewed as breakfast, not members of the family, but here were the two of them living together. An unlikely pair but an encouraging picture.

There's a bit in the Bible about wolves living with lambs, and lions eating straw – it's a dream of what the ideal world would be like. Translated into human terms, it's a vision of people renouncing violence, turning our swords into ploughs, and trying to solve our problems peacefully. Looking at today's world, we're a long way from that, but we have to dream. We need to hold on to a vision of what could be, if only we tried harder.

And it is hard. The story of the lioness and the antelope had its downside. Apparently one day another lion came along – a male, it would be, wouldn't it? – who didn't have quite the same feelings for the antelope. He ate it.

But would you believe it, the lioness did the same thing again. She found and befriended another orphaned antelope. There are always setbacks in life, whether it's Belfast or Jerusalem. But we go on hoping and praying; that's what makes us human. Let's keep doing it.

24

Lord of my dreams, I look to you today and everyday.
Open my heart to hope, and let me share my life with you.

Extract from Love is a Wild Bird, *first published 2003.*

Milli has a friend to stay

For in this hope we were saved. But hope that is seen is no hope at all.
Who hopes for what he already has? But if we hope for what we do not yet have,
we wait for it patiently.
Romans 8:24-25

Our dog, Milli, has had a friend staying with us – Toby, our daughter's dog. Milli's small and black. He's large, black and hairy. They get on well together but at feeding time we keep them at a distance. We put Milli's food in its usual place, but Toby's at the other end of our fairly large kitchen. The separation's important. Toby could eat for England in the Dog Olympics and come back with a medal. It takes him about eight seconds to hoover up everything in his bowl and then he looks over towards Milli. She's slower and has only just finished sniffing her food and deciding which bit she'll eat first, when he saunters over in her direction. He's not aggressive; he just hangs around in case anything gets left over.

The funny thing is that when Milli's finished her food she does the same thing in reverse – goes over to Toby's bowl on the off-chance he's left something. Neither dog ever leaves a crumb, but they're hopeful that this time it'll be different. It never is but they live and hope.

Or should it be hope and live? I was interviewed recently for a magazine article. I was asked, "When you were ten years old, what did you want to be when you were grown up?" "Alive," I answered. We can't really live without hope can we? Whether we live in Nottingham or West Sudan, it's only hope that keeps us going.

Lord of my future, I can do the hope,
but patience wears a little thin at times.
I need the help that only you can give.

Extract from Chasing the Leaves, *first published 2003.*

A. D. ASKEW

Frantic barking

Be completely humble and gentle;
be patient, bearing with one another in love.
Ephesians 4:2

Our little dog, Milli, protects us from harm. That's her view, anyway. We have a fairly big garden and every morning she rushes out to check it. The other day, the early morning quiet was shattered. Milli was barking frantically. I rushed out to quieten her. We have good neighbours but I wasn't sure how they'd enjoy being woken up at a quarter past six.

There was Milli, running from side to side like a collie herding sheep. But it wasn't sheep, it was a fox. Milli had it cornered. I think that the fox could really have made a meal of Milli, but it just stood there with its back to the hedge. My sudden appearance changed the balance. It couldn't stand the two of us and with a graceful leap the fox found a hole in the hedge and was off.

And Milli? A last growl and she came to tell me how tough she was. I wasn't quite as sure as Milli. I don't think confrontation is always the best way to deal with a crisis. There are other, quieter ways of defending our personal territory.

And, if we try, we can usually accommodate the other person, even if they have a different opinion from ours. It's worth the effort anyway. And, who knows, maybe they're right.

Lord, if I could only think before I growl,
listen before I shout, see the good
and offer space and dignity to those with whom I disagree.

Extract from Chasing the Leaves, *first published 2003.*

Flying hooligans

Praise be to the God and Father of our Lord Jesus Christ,
who has blessed us in the heavenly realms
with every spiritual blessing in Christ.
Ephesians 1:3

They came in formation, flying low across the water. I could almost hear the Dam Busters' theme playing in the background, but the noise was the Canada geese. They were honking to announce their arrival at the nature reserve and to clear the runway for landing. They came in; heads high, tails down, wings arched, and hit the water with a flurry, one after the other.

I never tire of watching them land – can you use the word 'land' when they're coming onto water? But the noise they make! Flying hooligans, big and strong and extrovert; I'm just glad they don't follow football.

One minute they're masters of the air, the next equally competent in water. And when they see the chance of food from human visitors they walk on land as well. Comfortable in all three elements. Most of us poor humans are okay on land, not-so-good in water, and the only way we can fly is by buying a ticket. Yet we have the greatest opportunity of all, to enjoy the greatest element of all – the spiritual. To open ourselves up to the imagination, to creativity, to the source which powers them all.

*Lord, open my eyes, ears and mind to the wonder of
your presence and make me sensitive to your Spirit.*

Extract from Dabbling with Ducks, *first published 2007.*

31

A brood of fledglings

Are not five sparrows sold for two pennies? Yet not one of them is forgotten
by God. Indeed, the very hairs of your head are all numbered.
Don't be afraid; you are worth more than many sparrows.
Luke 12:6–7

And the kingdom of heaven is like this: we asked a local carpenter to put in two new
wooden gateposts. He said he'd buy them, soak them in creosote to preserve them,
and then come and do the job.

We waited. Nothing happened. Then he phoned. "Sorry for the delay," he said.
"I soaked the posts and put them in the back of my workshop to dry. When
I went to get them I found a pair of blackbirds had made a nest on them, and now
there's a brood of fledgelings there. I haven't the heart to disturb them. I'll come
when they've flown."

We agreed, happily. It's a little thing, but how reassuring to find a man with values
like that. Our culture is so profit-orientated, so geared to money, that nothing else
seems to matter.

Here, in a small way, is someone saying that life matters, however small the dividend
seems. There are other values besides gain, values which bring richness to life,
richness beyond riches.

Incidentally, when the birds had flown and he came to do the work, he brought the
nest to show us. The marks of the posts were clear to see. Just a family of small,
common birds, but I think Jesus would have made a parable out of the story.

Lord, give me the carpenter's sympathy and love for little things.
Help me to find value in the undervalued
and to find worth in things without a price tag.

Extract from Facing the Storm, *first published 1989.*

All it needed, Lord, was a little time.
A bit of patience. A few more days.
But it would have been so easy to disturb the nest.
"I need the wood for a gate," he could have said.
"What's all the fuss about?"
And trampled on the future.

It's so easy to ignore the little things.
Things with no voice, no influence.
No strings to pull.
The small and insignificant.
And yet, Lord, saying that is judgement I've no right to make.
Small and insignificant to whom?
No sparrow falls, you said, without God knowing.
You, like the carpenter, concerned for little things.
You, as a carpenter, caring that the least
should find a place of value in your kingdom.
A kingdom for the poor and weak.
If influence found favour in your sight,
if privilege bought places in your kingdom,
there'd be a lot of empty places there.

And when I look at me,
I'm glad your kingdom takes the weak and struggling.
For that gives me a chance.
I stand renewed in hope.

Stand confident,
not in the righteousness I sometimes kid myself about –
just puffed up feathers on a frosty morning –
but in your wide compassion.

And in response, Lord,
give me a ready understanding, for all who have no power.
Give me the carpenter's sympathy and love for little things.
Help me find value in the undervalued,
find worth in things without a price tag.

I like to think that the carpenter, one day,
may share a glance with you, Lord,
one carpenter to another,
Because he shared your love of little things.
And if the gateposts of your kingdom should ever need repairing
Perhaps you'll think of him.

Paddling and dabbling

I keep asking that the God of our Lord Jesus Christ,
the glorious Father, may give you the Spirit of wisdom
and revelation, so that you may know him better.
Ephesians 1:17

After the honking of the Canada geese, the ducks flew in, quieter, gentler. Mallards, the females smart but modest in tawny brown, although flashing – forgive the word – a small wing patch of blue and white. The males showier, lovely iridescent blue-green heads, deep-brown chest, and the blue and white on their wings too.

They fly in over the water, wings high, producing an air resistance that slows them to stalling speed. Then, they lower their undercarriage and, braced for contact, they skim the water and land with a gentle splash. Then they paddle into shallow water and suddenly upend themselves, head and shoulders under water, only the tail visible, pointing to the sky, and two pink feet paddling to stabilise the whole balancing act. Not the most elegant position.

Dabbling, it's called. I thought that was a made-up word out of a children's story – used in *The Wind in the Willows* actually – but it's a serious word used to classify ducks. They're either divers or dabblers, depending on how they look for food. Dabblers upend and graze on water plants that grow just below the surface. Divers – well, that's obvious.

Maybe we should dabble a bit more. Try to get below the surface of life and take hold of some of the possibilities that could open up if we just went a little bit deeper. And, who knows, maybe one day we'll be ready to dive.

Unfathomable Lord,
the deeper I dive below the surface of life,
the nearer I get to your love.

Extract from Dabbling with Ducks, *first published 2007.*

The bird seed takeaway

Are not two sparrows sold for a penny? Yet not one of them
will fall to the ground apart from the will of your Father.
Matthew 10:29

I'd filled the bird feeder with a mix of seeds and nuts and was watching through the kitchen window. There are fewer birds in the garden these days, but there were sparrows squabbling, a blackbird, one lonely starling – where have all the others gone? – and a chaffinch. The collared doves and pigeons had found another takeaway for the morning.

As I watched, I suddenly realised that those birds didn't have the faintest idea of who'd put the seed there. They didn't even realise that someone had to put it out. For them, the seed's just there. And they never say thank you. They just eat. My satisfaction comes from seeing them there, and knowing I've done just a tiny bit to help them through another winter's day. And that's all I need.

When you think about it, we humans are the only living creatures in the world who can say "thank you". We may think our family dogs do, but that look in Milli's eye when I give her a Choc Drop is less a "thank you", more a "Have you got another one for me?" expression. So, if we are the only living creatures with enough language to allow us to use the word, let's use it a bit more. Thank you for reading.

Generous Lord, my gratitude's not always up to scratch.
Forgive, and take the desire for the deed.

Extract from Dabbling with Ducks, *first published 2007.*

Koko and the kitten

A shoot will come up from the stump of Jesse;
from his roots a Branch will bear fruit.
The Spirit of the LORD will rest on him –
the Spirit of wisdom and of understanding,
the Spirit of counsel and of might,
the Spirit of the knowledge and fear of the LORD –
and he will delight in the fear of the LORD.
...
The wolf will live with the lamb, the leopard will lie down with the goat,
the calf and the lion and the yearling together; and a little child will lead them.
The cow will feed with the bear, their young will lie down together,
and the lion will eat straw like the ox.
The infant will play near the cobra's den,
and the young child will put its hand into the viper's nest.
They will neither harm nor destroy on all my holy mountain,
for the earth will be filled with the knowledge of the LORD
as the waters cover the sea.
Isaiah 11:1-3, 6-9

I saw a fascinating news report. Koko, a gorilla weighing more than 300 pounds, had taken a kitten as a pet. It happened in California. Shortly after Koko was born, a psychologist took over her upbringing, and began to teach her a sign language developed for the deaf.

Over 12 years Koko has learnt, and uses, more than 500 words and signs. Some time ago, she signed that she wanted a kitten – she'd been shown pictures of them. The psychologist gave her a woolly toy kitten. Koko rejected it and asked for a real one. I have some lovely photographs of the result – this great gorilla cradling her tiny pet with great tenderness.

Some years ago I visited Lambarene, the hospital created by Albert Schweitzer, in Gabon. There I befriended a baby gorilla, an orphan of about three months, its mother having been shot by a hunter. I've never known an animal so in need of affection. We would sometimes play together, but more often it would just cling to me, holding tight. There were problems. At only three months it weighed about 40 pounds, and it could cling with both hands and feet. It was difficult to disengage.

The behaviour of these two animals set me thinking. Misunderstood as savage, dangerous animals, 'all they need is love' to paraphrase a song by the Beatles. Part of the problem is that we stereotype both animals and people. We latch on to one characteristic and over-emphasise it. "Foxes are cunning," we say, "lions are fierce." With humans we classify a whole nationality as noisy, arrogant or mean. We do it with individuals, too. We say a co-worker is uncooperative or difficult. We close our minds and look no further. We believe our own prejudices and never try to change things. Now here is Koko, a gorilla, quietly breaking our assumptions. Learning a language, communicating and showing elements of tenderness. How different from the stereotype. Maybe, dare I suggest it, we should apply this insight to the 'gorillas' we work or live with! If we dropped our prejudices maybe we'd find tenderness in them too, under the surface.

Perhaps there's a weakness in my argument. Koko was born in a zoo. Maybe you could argue that she's not normal, she's never had to face the threat of harsh life in the forest. True, but she still has her instincts – they can't be bred out in one generation. So maybe there's another thought here: if human beings could be brought up in an environment where threats and violence were not accepted as a part of common life, maybe they'd grow up loving, too!.

Extract from Many Voices, One Voice, *first published 1985.*

Lord God, Creator,
all life is yours.
All that has come to be
has come through you.
Lives in your energy,
takes breath because you willed it.
Is clothed in your beauty,
your dignity.
Part of your world.
Valued and loved.

Lord, I too am a creator.
My shallow judgment
creates deep prejudice.
My lazy assumptions
conceive misunderstanding.
My lack of love brings misery to birth.

Teach me, Lord, to love what you have created.
Help me to shed the arrogance that cocoons me
and restricts my growth.
Help me to split the binding threads
and crawl out into the warmth of your light.
Stretch the wings of my understanding.

Teach me to see people
one by one.
Not to pigeonhole them, categorise.
Not to hammer them into unnatural moulds
of my own making.
But to rejoice in every difference.
To accept people as they are.
Each one a part of your creation.
Showing something of your glory.

At times, Lord,
I meet people
I can see no good in.
No glory.
No redeeming feature.
Lord, is that true?
Or is it just my eyes?

Milli and the nest of tables

*Instead, speaking the truth in love, we will in all things
grow up into him who is the Head, that is, Christ.*
Ephesians 4:15

The shortest way between two points is a straight line – unless you live in the deep rain forest in New Guinea, which is so thick it's hardly possible to walk in a straight line. Large trees get in the way, and local people have little idea of the concept.

But our dog, Milli, believes in the idea, particularly indoors. In strategic places in our sitting room are small occasional tables – a nest of tables, smaller ones fitting under the larger. They're past their sell-by-date really, we bought them years ago, and they're a bit rickety. But if a table's in Milli's way she walks straight through it.

That's okay if it's the largest, there's room for her to get through underneath, and there are usually a couple of heavy books on top which keeps it stable. But when she walks under a smaller table she upends it and takes it with her. Make sure you're holding your coffee mug at the time.

A straight line between two points isn't necessarily the best when it comes to talking either. Tact and kindness may be preferable to blunt disagreement. Wrong words can upset the apple cart, or the occasional table. Some folk say that with straight words at least we know exactly where we are with people – but it's not necessarily where we want to be.

*Gentle Lord, help me to think before I speak,
and then say little.*

Extract from Dabbling with Ducks, *first published 2007.*

44

Graceful pirouettes

The Word became flesh and made his dwelling among us.
We have seen his glory . . .
John 1:14

Whenever I watch wildlife programmes on television I think of David Attenborough. He's made us so conscious of the world of nature and its wonders. Someone said that when he dies he should be put in a shoe box and buried at the bottom of the garden with the hamsters, but that's another story.

Recently I watched a programme on grey whales. Their beauty left me speechless - for a moment anyway - their twists and turns, their graceful pirouettes as they swam in and out of the picture, now close up, now disappearing into the green depths of the water.

The commentator admitted that their lives are still very private and that we know little about them. He finished by saying, "Maybe it's good that there are things we don't know. We need to keep the mystery of life."

Whatever the subject, we want to know more. That's what science is about, observing and recording, satisfying our curiosity, adding to the knowledge we already have. And that's fine, but every time we find an answer it seems to raise more questions.

The mystery's still there. Reminding us that we can never know everything, because the source, the prime mover in creation, is that power we call God. A God whom we believe is revealed to us in Jesus Christ, but even here the mystery remains. However much we know of him, there's more to learn, more to experience.

There's a time to measure and analyse, but there's also a time to sit back, accept, and say, "Thank you."

Extract from Slower than Butterflies, *first published 1997.*

Ever-loving Lord, thank you seems so small a phrase
yet it's the only one I've got for what I feel. I'll try to use it more.

A flurry of feathers

But I trust in your unfailing love; my heart rejoices in your
salvation. I will sing to the Lord, for he has been good to me.
Psalm 13:5-6

I went through the nature reserve the other day. It was cold and the trees seemed to
huddle together for warmth. As I walked I heard a snatch of bird song. Then a flicker
of movement in a bush grabbed my attention. I stood still and waited. Another
movement and a flash of red. Just a robin.

He watched me, head tilted, alert, ready to fly. Slowly, I felt for a piece of bread crust
in my pocket. Then, even more slowly, with no sudden movement, I stretched my
arm out with the bread in my open hand. And waited. The robin hopped onto a
nearer branch and watched. I waited some more. We both, the robin and I,
concentrated on the bread. He hopped nearer, just out of reach.

Then he committed himself. With a flurry of feathers he landed on my hand, almost
weightless, took the bread and was off again. He didn't wait to say thank you – or did
he? I felt privileged. That moment of trust was thanks enough. Trust takes time to
build. The confidence to trust someone doesn't happen in a flash. It's an act of faith.
In trust we surrender something of ourselves to another person. It can be risky, but it
enriches life.

And that was it. Our encounter was over. The robin flew away with his piece of
bread. I went away with a smile on my face, my day brightened by a flash of red,
a snatch of bird song, and a moment of trust.

*Lord, help me to trust today;
to take the bread of life your hand holds out to me.*

Extract from Love is a Wild Bird, *first published 2003.*

Chimpanzees and humans

*So God created human beings in his own image,
in the image of God he created them;
male and female he created them.
God saw all that he had made, and it was very good.*
Genesis 1:27, 31

Scientists have been comparing the genetic code – DNA – of chimpanzees and humans. We're told they're nearly the same. Estimates vary but they're between 95 per cent and 99 per cent identical. In one sense it's not surprising – every living thing on Planet Earth, animal, vegetable or human, has to use the same basic elements for its make-up.

But if it concerns you to be associated so closely with chimpanzees, I suggest that, looking at the way some human beings behave these days, it should worry the chimps even more to be linked closely with us. And I reckon the most important thing isn't the similarity, but the 5 per cent or 1 per cent difference.

The little extras that make us human. I'm thinking of the good and positive things. The sense of justice that makes us protest at unfairness and inequality. The goodwill that makes people respond so generously when disaster strikes. The love and understanding that motivate so many of our relationships. We can look at it all negatively when we see some people reverting to the jungle in their behaviour, but the great thing is that goodness survives, and tends to break out when it's most needed.

And if I can find a little gene for that in my make-up, then I'll settle for my closeness to the apes.

Lord of all goodness, I'm only human,
but that is all you want of me;
to walk with you and grow in grace.

Extract from Chasing the Leaves, *first published 2003.*

The puppy who liked pebbles

*"For there is nothing hidden that will not be disclosed,
and nothing concealed that will not be known or brought
out into the open."*
Luke 8:17

There was a report in the newspaper recently about a woman and her pet dog. Every time she stroked it she felt there was something strange about its stomach. Then she heard a noise when she touched it – not the usual puppy sounds – something different, a sort of scrunching noise. She took the dog to the vet. He too was puzzled. He anaesthetised the dog and took X-rays. All was revealed.

In the dog's stomach were 32 pebbles which he'd picked up and eaten. No one knows why – except the dog, and he's not telling – but it could give a new meaning to the phrase 'being stoned'.

Seriously, you never know what's going on beneath the surface, do you? Whether it's animal or human there's a lot more to us than meets the eye. On the surface everything may look alright. "No problem," we say, but people often cover up their anxieties, pretend they're OK when really they're crying out for help. That doesn't give us the right to probe around in other people's lives but it may make us a little slower to criticise and judge. And it may suggest that we should spread our friendship around more. Include more people in it.

A bit more sympathy with other folk's behaviour will make the day a little better. And incidentally, the puppy made a full recovery.

Lord, when I think I have the answer, maybe I'm asking the wrong question. Lend me a little of your understanding as I live today.

Extract from Love is a Wild Bird, *first published 2003.*

The brave squirrel

By faith Abraham, when called to go to a place he would later
receive as his inheritance, obeyed and went, even though he did
not know where he was going.

Hebrews 11:8

Grey squirrels look very attractive bouncing around the garden, but they lost their
popularity with me when one of them chewed its way into our loft. It caused several
hundred pounds worth of damage biting through electric cables. The house insurance
didn't cover it – squirrels are classed as vermin. Read the small print.

But yesterday I watched one squirrel in the garden. He was on the flat roof of a
garage just the other side of our hawthorn hedge. He was a bit agitated, running one
way, then another. Suddenly he took a massive leap, out and up, to the branch of a
tree that must have been ten feet away. An enormous jump for such a small animal.
He made it – just. Then with a twitch of his bushy tail he was away into new territory.

I don't know why he jumped. Maybe he'd been scared by something I couldn't see.
Perhaps he saw an opportunity ahead of him. Whatever it was he had the courage to
take a leap of faith. To move on from where he was. A leap into the unknown, into
the future.

When we're faced with problems we all have to make decisions. Even not making a
decision is a decision in itself, if you see what I mean, and it's not always easy. But we
all have to move on. When circumstances change or new opportunities arrive we
need to do something. It can take courage. We can't be sure how things will turn out,
but we need to take a deep breath and jump. Fortunately God's always around
waiting to help.

Extract from Love is a Wild Bird, *first published 2003.*

Lord of the future,
hold out your hands
and catch me
when I jump.

Suddenly Divine

The following is an extract from Eddie's memoirs, Edge of Daylight,
*which describes his years working as Superintendent at
Purulia Leprosy Home and Hospital in West Bengal, India.*

When the sheep stole the show

Most of our development was without electricity. There was a small and erratic electricity supply company in Purulia town but it was functioning at its limit with old generators and we were too far out of town anyway. It would have been too expensive to pay for several miles of posts and overhead wires to the hospital. But it was hard running a hospital without it. There was no power for X-ray machines, only hurricane lanterns in the wards and pressure lamps in the operating theatre and elsewhere.

Then came a State Government project bringing power from a new dam built 40 miles away. We watched with growing anticipation as the line of pylons gradually snaked across the fields. It passed less than a mile from the hospital and after battling through a morass of red tape we were able to make a connection. It made a great difference. Proper lighting everywhere. Power for X-ray, air conditioning in the major operating theatre and much more.

We always staged a nativity play at Christmas. It was a joint effort by staff and patients, adults and children. When our first Christmas with electricity came, we decided the play would be the biggest and the best we'd ever put on. It would be out in the open air and in the evening so that we could make full use of the new lighting. We built an earth stage on a wide stretch of flat ground and erected a makeshift proscenium arch over it, all bamboo and jute sacking. We made footlights out of old kerosene tins and lined them across the stage.

In the planning group someone said, "As it's outside let's have a real fire for the shepherds to sit around." It was a great idea which began to expand under its own impetus. "What about real sheep?" That was easy. We could borrow a dozen from the nearby village. And although we didn't recognise it that's where the trouble began.

In rehearsal the sheep began to stray looking for food. We chopped up straw for them and spread it around on the ground. They ate it quickly and strayed some more. Then came another idea. "Let's tie string around the necks of the sheep and each shepherd can hold two or three of them. The strings won't be seen in the dark." It seemed to work.

My idea was the one that did it. Near the stage was the central kitchen. It had a flat roof. I suggested that we put up a ladder against the far side of the kitchen. The angels, all children in white robes and silver wings, could climb up quietly in the dark and line up on the roof edge. At the appropriate moment we could switch on the floodlights, kept in reserve for the occasion. The angels would suddenly appear as though flying through the dark night sky, the stars behind them. It was high drama.

Came the evening of the play. The air was taut with excitement. Almost all the patients gathered, Hindu, Muslim, Christian. The staff were there in force and so were many folk from the neighbouring villages. There was just one thing we hadn't taken into account in our planning. That was the sheep's reaction when the lights suddenly flashed on and the angels appeared from nowhere. The stage was flooded in light and so was the heavenly host. "Baaa," went the sheep. "Fear not," shouted the angels from on high. "Baaaa," went the sheep. "We bring you good tidings of great joy," shouted the angels. In Bengali of course. "Baaaaa," went the sheep and one, even more terrified than the rest, backed into the fire.

And there were shepherds living out in the fields near by,
keeping watch over their flocks at night.
An angel of the Lord appeared to them,
and the glory of the Lord shone around them,
and they were terrified. But the angel said to them,
'Do not be afraid, I bring you good news
that will cause great joy for all the people.'
Luke 2:8–10

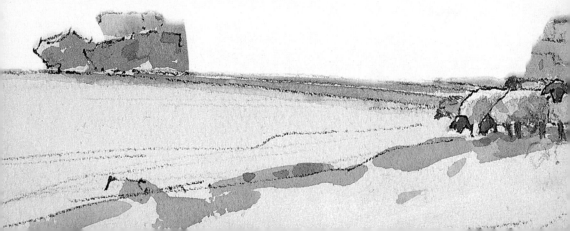

Its tail began to burn. It bleated once more, jumped about a foot in the air, wrenched its string from the shepherd's restraining hand and leapt into the dark. All the other sheep followed. Within seconds there were a dozen panic-stricken sheep dashing through an audience of a thousand people sitting cross-legged in the dark. It was pandemonium. Some made valiant attempts to catch the sheep, grasping wildly as living legs of mutton dashed by. It was in vain. It took us almost 24 hours to track down the last sheep. I don't remember how we finished the play. My mind has blanked it out. It wasn't the best nativity play we ever produced but it's the one we all remember.

Extract from Edge of Daylight, *first published 2000.*

Lord, help me to step out in faith today.
Ready to use my energies for you.
In hope. In confidence. With joy.

The following is an extract from Eddie's memoirs, Edge of Daylight, *describing life at home in India*

Family pets

We had great fun at home. We were into pets as a family. I acquired two Rhesus monkeys. One was a large mature male who only stayed with us a couple of days. We hoped he'd acclimatise but on his second night he made a successful jailbreak. With a colleague and a net from the hospital goal posts, I spent a morning trying to catch him but he loved our flat roofs and the drain pipes were a delight to him. He'd watch every move we made until we clambered up our ladders and slowly approached him. Then, when we were only yards away, he'd casually unfold his limbs and leap effortlessly into the nearest tree. He was fast and far more athletic than we were. Our last sighting of him was up a tree in the local Christian cemetery. Then he disappeared.

The other monkey was small, young and beautiful. An expressive pink face, round liquid-brown eyes. We named him Squeak because that's what he did. When not at large or sitting on my shoulder he lived on the end of a very long light chain. It had a metal ring at the other end which slid loosely up and down an eight-foot pole with a boxy house for him at the top. It gave him freedom of movement and a place of safety from stray dogs. Not that he needed it.

He befriended a neighbour's dog, a substantial and portly black mongrel named Gagarin. The USSR had recently launched him into space. The original cosmonaut Gagarin, not the dog. The two animals spent time together and Squeak was often seen perched on Gagarin's back going for a ride.

Squeak was fascinated by the geese we kept. He found a weak link in his chain, freed himself and went to investigate. There was a great honking and hissing and Squeak appeared, a goose egg under his arm, making a mad dash round the garden like a rugger three-quarter going for the line. The geese were not amused but he was too fast for them.

Sometime later we were woken very early in the morning by distress calls and a crashing in the trees. I got up. Squeak was not where he should have been. He called. I looked around. He was about twenty feet up a tree at the end of the garden, the loose end of his chain snagged inextricably on the spur of a branch. He was stuck. I began to climb the tree in my pyjamas. I moved out towards him, hanging with my arms and legs wrapped around the branch he was attached to. I got closer and tried with one hand to untangle the chain. He edged nearer muttering to himself. Finally he let go of the branch and sat on my head. He leaned forward until his face was upside down and within two inches of mine. "This is a fine mess you've got us into," I heard him say, although the family wouldn't believe it when I told them later.

Lord, help me to seize the day, to shake it 'til the joy it holds spills out and fills my life.

Eddie and Squeak, Purulia, c. 1963

How many are your works, LORD!
In wisdom you made them all;
the earth is full of your creatures.
Psalm 104:24

Lord God, Creator, all life is yours.
All that has come to be
has come through you.
Lives in your energy,
takes breath because you willed it.
Is clothed in your beauty, your dignity.
Part of your world. Valued and loved.